P9-DIY-920

WHAT ARE the ARTICLES OF CONFEDERATION?

And Other Questions about the Birth of the United States

Laura Hamilton Waxman

LERNER PUBLICATIONS COMPANY · MINNEAPOLIS

A Word about Language

English word usage, spelling, grammar, and punctuation have changed over the centuries. We have preserved original spellings and word usage in the quotations included in this book.

Lerner Publications Company
A division of Lerner Publishing Group, Inc.
241 First Avenue North
Minneapolis, MN 55401 U.S.A.

Website address: www.lernerbooks.com

Library of Congress Cataloging-in-Publication Data

Waxman, Laura Hamilton.
    What are the Articles of Confederation? : and other questions about the birth of
the United States / by Laura Hamilton Waxman.
        p.   cm. — (Six questions of American history)
    Includes bibliographical references and index.
    ISBN 978–0–7613–5330–0 (lib. bdg. : alk. paper)
    1. United States. Articles of Confederation—Juvenile literature. 2. Constitutional
history—United States—Juvenile literature. 3. United States—Politics and
government—1775–1783—Juvenile literature. 4. United States—Politics and
government—1783–1789—Juvenile literature. I. Title.
KF4508.W39 2012
342.7302'9—dc23   2011018032

Manufactured in the United States of America
1 – DP – 12/31/11

TABLE OF CONTENTS 4

THE SIX
QUESTIONS
HELP YOU
DISCOVER THE
FACTS!

INTRODUCTION

In the summer of 1776, a group of men traveled to Philadelphia, Pennsylvania, from all over the United States. There, they sat in a stuffy meeting hall, arguing with one another. While they fought, American soldiers fought too. The soldiers were battling the British army in the Revolutionary War (1775–1783). At stake was the freedom of the newly formed United States of America.

Far from the booming cannons, the group of men hammered out their nation's future. They had declared their freedom from Great Britain. But they still needed to set up a new government. During those hot summer months, they worked on the Articles of Confederation. This important document would set down rules for the nation's government. The men clashed over many questions. Should the national government have more power than the states? Or should it have less? How would it get enough money and soldiers to win the war? Should the large states have a greater voice in the government? Or should all states have the same power? The disagreements and quarrels went on and on.

By the end of the summer, the men had grown frustrated and discouraged. Yet they *had* to find a solution. Without a government, the country could never hope to win the war. And if it didn't win the war, it wouldn't survive as an independent country. What had Great Britain done to anger the Americans?

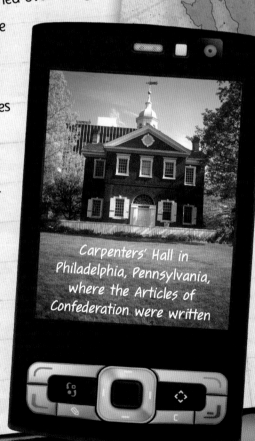

Carpenters' Hall in Philadelphia, Pennsylvania, where the Articles of Confederation were written

THE THIRTEEN COLONIES 1763-1783

BRITISH TERRITORY (CANADA)

GREAT LAKES

LAKE SUPERIOR

MISSISSIPPI RIVER

LAKE HURON

LAKE MICHIGAN

LAKE ERIE

OHIO RIVER

LAKE ONTARIO

ST. LAWRENCE RIVER

DISTRICT OF MAINE (PART OF MA)

LEXINGTON

NEW YORK

CONCORD

NEW HAMPSHIRE

MASSACHUSETTS

BOSTON

BOSTON HARBOR

RHODE ISLAND

CONNECTICUT

PENNSYLVANIA

DELAWARE RIVER

NEW YORK CITY

PHILADELPHIA

NEW JERSEY

DELAWARE

BALTIMORE

MARYLAND

RICHMOND

VIRGINIA

CHESAPEAKE BAY

NORTH CAROLINA

SOUTH CAROLINA

GEORGIA

SPANISH TERRITORY

BRITISH TERRITORY

ORIGINAL THIRTEEN COLONIES

N

GULF OF MEXICO

NORTH ATLANTIC OCEAN

U.S. artist Alonzo Chappell (1828–1887) painted the Battle of Lexington (1775), the first battle of the American Revolution. American colonists sought to free themselves from British rule.

5

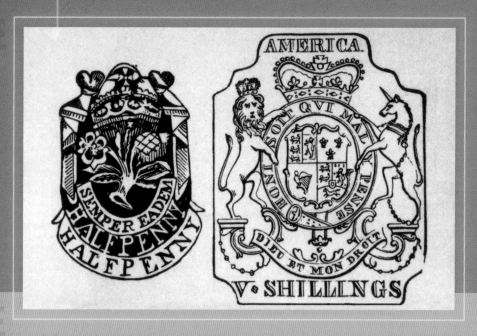

Here are two of the stamps that Americans had to buy from Great Britain during the Stamp Act.

SEMPER EADEM
HALF PENNY
HALF PENNY

AMERICA
HONI SOIT QVI MAL Y PENSE
DIEU ET MON DROIT
V. SHILLINGS

ONE GOING TO WAR

lands under the control of a foreign country

Great Britain had ruled its thirteen eastern colonies in eastern North America for more than one hundred years. The colonies had enjoyed the protection of the world's most powerful nation. They also enjoyed having control over their own governments. The colonial governments raised their own taxes. They made their own laws.

The peaceful relationship between Britain and its colonies began to change in 1765. Britain's Parliament passed the Stamp Act. It taxed

the lawmaking body of Great Britain's government

everything from newspapers to playing cards. All these items required an official British stamp.

6

WHY DID BRITAIN START TAXING THE COLONIES?

British colonists were not the only people living in North America. Native Americans had lived on the land for thousands of years. France and Spain also claimed neighboring colonies. Tensions over borders often arose among these groups. In 1754 the French and Indian War broke out between the British and the French. Certain Native American communities sided with the French, while others supported the British. American colonists fought on Britain's side. Britain won the war in 1763 but at great cost. Its government needed to pay for the expensive war. Britain's Parliament passed the Stamp Act to raise money from the colonies.

The stamp cost money. Unlike colonial taxes, Stamp Act money didn't go to the colonies. It went to the British government 3,000 miles (4,830 kilometers) away.

The Stamp Act angered many colonists. They argued that Parliament had no right to tax them.

This painting shows British solders attacking Native Americans during the French and Indian War (1754–1763). British soldiers were known as redcoats due to their red uniforms.

The colonists said that citizens in Britain had representatives in Parliament. But the colonists did not. That meant the colonists did not have a voice or a vote in Parliament. They couldn't vote yes or no on taxes. Therefore, the colonists argued, Parliament shouldn't be allowed to tax them.

Colonial leaders published letters and essays laying out their arguments. They hoped Britain's king and its lawmakers would listen. Parliament ended the Stamp Act in 1766. But it replaced it with new taxes on paint, glass, paper, and tea. People throughout the colonies protested these taxes too.

The protests were especially strong in Boston, Massachusetts. Britain sent soldiers to the city to silence the colonists. It also passed laws to control

Residents of New York burned stamps to protest the Stamp Act in 1765.

WHO WAS KING GEORGE III?

King George III (right) was born in England in 1738. He ruled Britain from 1760 until his death in 1820. King George was not elected by the people of Britain. Like earlier British rulers, he was born into power. His grandfather had been King George II. When George II died, George III automatically became the next king. Many Americans believed King George was a cruel and unfair ruler. They hoped to find a different way to choose their leaders.

Massachusetts in other ways. The message was loud and clear. Britain's powerful government would punish any colony that fought against its laws.

In April 1775, a battle broke out between colonists and British soldiers. It took place in Massachusetts. This battle marked the start of the Revolutionary War.

Members from each of the thirteen colonies traveled to Carpenters' Hall in Philadelphia, Pennsylvania, to participate in the Second Continental Congress.

people chosen by a colony or a state to represent its needs and wishes

The next month, delegates from the thirteen colonies met in Philadelphia. The meeting was called the Second Continental Congress. There the delegates discussed what the colonies should do next.

Radicals, such as Samuel Adams of Boston, wanted

people in favor of basic changes

independence. These men and women believed the colonies should break free from Great Britain. They wanted to form a separate nation.

people who
want to
keep things
as they are

Conservatives, such as John Dickinson from Pennsylvania, had other ideas. They hoped the colonies could make peace with Britain. Dickinson was famous for his popular *Letters from a Farmer in Pennsylvania*. In these essays, he argued that the colonies alone had the power to tax themselves. But he and other conservatives were loyal to Britain. They wanted the two sides to solve their disagreements peacefully.

Dickinson and other conservatives feared that the colonies couldn't survive on their own. After all, Dickinson argued, it was only Great Britain that held the colonies together. People in the different colonies didn't know how to work together. And they didn't really trust one another. He wondered how they could form a successful nation.

Benjamin Franklin of Philadelphia agreed that forming a new nation would be hard. The colonies were "not only under different governors," he said. They "have different forms of government [and] different laws." He added that some of them had different customs and religions too.

John Dickinson

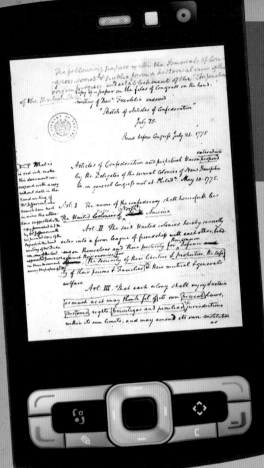

This handwritten version of the Articles of Confederation by Benjamin Franklin was presented to the Continental Congress in 1775. In it, Franklin outlined his plan to bring the individual colonies together as one.

But Franklin believed the colonies would have to unite to stand a chance against Britain. After all, Great Britain had the most powerful army in the world.

Franklin wrote a plan to form a confederation of the colonies. He called his plan *Sketch of Articles of Confederation*. Franklin named the confederation the United Colonies of America. His plan showed how to form a confederation government.

confederation | a union of colonies, states, or nations

The Continental Congress rejected Franklin's plan. Radicals weren't interested in forming a new government. They only wanted to organize an army and win the war. Conservatives thought it was too soon to start thinking about a confederation.

But many conservatives changed their minds after a year of war. They realized that Britain wasn't interested in making peace. This saddened men such as John Dickinson. "We...love our mother country," he said. But "her sword is opening our veins."

The Continental Congress met again in the summer of 1776. Many delegates wanted the colonies to declare their independence from Britain right away. Conservative delegates agreed that the colonies needed to separate from Britain. But they pleaded with the Congress to slow down. They believed that the colonies should first come together as a confederation. To do this, the delegates needed to write and agree on the Articles of Confederation.

On June 11, Congress asked Thomas Jefferson of Virginia to lead a new committee. Its job was to draft the Declaration of Independence. The next day, Congress asked John Dickinson to lead another committee. That committee's job was to draft the Articles of Confederation. Both men were respected thinkers and writers. Both had reputations as honest leaders. And both men cared deeply about the colonies. As they took up their pens, they took the future of the colonies into their hands.

NEXT QUESTION

WHEN DID CONGRESS BEGIN DISCUSSING THE ARTICLES OF CONFEDERATION?

Thomas Jefferson reads his draft of the Declaration of Independence to Benjamin Franklin in 1776.

TWO DRAFTING THE ARTICLES

Dickinson used many of Franklin's ideas in his own plan. As he worked, he showed the document to his committee. The group had one delegate from each colony. Some men were conservatives. Some were radicals. Others were in the middle. Because of these differences, the men argued about almost every detail. Committee member Josiah Bartlett complained, "I fear it will take some time before it will be finally settled."

By the end of June, Jefferson had finished the Declaration of Independence. Congress planned to vote on it in early July. On July 1, Dickinson stood before

Congress to plead for more time. He believed the colonies should first agree on the Articles of Confederation. Then they could declare independence. That way they would have a central government in place before becoming a new nation.

Most of the delegates disagreed with Dickinson. They approved the Declaration the next day. They proclaimed July 4 as the official day of independence for "the united States of America."

Dickinson refused to vote for or sign the Declaration. In fact, he decided to leave Congress. Working on the Articles had worn him out. He knew his opinions had made him unpopular.

Dickinson's committee showed the Articles of Confederation to Congress on July 12. The delegates debated the Articles for the rest of that steamy summer. They kept the windows closed even in the heat. The delegates wanted to keep their plans a secret from the British.

WHO WAS JOHN DICKINSON?

John Dickinson was a successful lawyer and respected lawmaker living in Philadelphia. His *Letters from a Farmer* had been printed in most newspapers in the colonies. He had also written a popular patriotic tune called the "Liberty Song." Dickinson's unpopular opinions about the Declaration of Independence made him give up his job as a Pennsylvania lawmaker. But he later served in Delaware, first as a lawmaker and then as governor. Dickinson also took part in later debates over the nation's future. He died in 1808 at the age of seventy-five.

Dickinson's draft set out plans for creating a "firm league of friendship"among the thirteen states. His Articles of Confederation called for a strong central government similar to Great Britain's. He and other conservatives believed the states needed such a government to keep them united.

Some delegates agreed with Dickinson's plan. But many others did not. They argued that a strong central government could misuse its power. Nobody wanted that, they said. They believed the states should have complete control over themselves. These delegates wanted a weak central government. They wanted it to have just enough power to run the war and keep peace among the states.

The delegates debated the Articles of Confederation all summer. Yet they returned to their states without an agreement. Over the next year, the delegates met several times. But they always struggled to find a compromise.

an argument ended by each side giving up something

Members of the Continental Congress discussed the Articles of Confederation in several meetings during 1776–1777.

In spring 1777, Thomas Burke suggested a new article. This one would protect the states' powers. The article began, "Each state retains its sovereignty, freedom, and independence, and every Power, Jurisdiction, and right."

The article said that the states would be like small nations. They would have total power and control over themselves. The central government would have no right to pass laws or raise taxes. It couldn't control trade between states. And it had no power to punish the states. This meant the central government couldn't force the states to do anything they didn't want to do. After some debate, the delegates agreed to this new article.

The delegates had a harder time agreeing on other important articles. The new Continental Army needed money, supplies, weapons, and soldiers to win the war. But the central government could not tax citizens directly. Everything had to come from the states. Some delegates thought that states with bigger populations should supply more. And states with fewer people should supply less. Other delegates wanted states with more land to give more. John Witherspoon of New Jersey had another idea.

trade the business of buying and selling goods

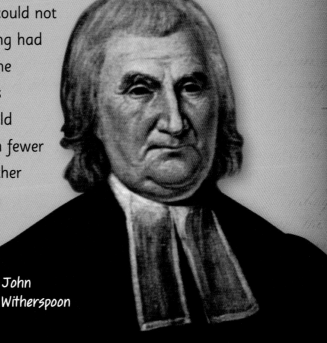

John
Witherspoon

Witherspoon said that each state should fund the Congress based on the value of its land. The government would first set up a fair system for determining that value. The delegates finally agreed to this idea.

Tempers also flared over how the states would vote on important decisions. Should the larger states get more votes? Or should every state have an equal vote? Massachusetts, Pennsylvania, and Virginia made up nearly half the nation's population. Delegates from those states thought they should get more votes. Those states also had the most valuable land. That meant they would have to supply more money and soldiers to the central government. So they should have a greater voice in the government, they said.

The smaller states strongly disagreed. They worried that the large states would take control of the central government. They hated that idea. They said they'd rather live under Britain's rule. Their argument won. The delegates agreed to give each state one vote.

The third problem proved to be the trickiest. Certain states had claimed land in the western territories. Virginia alone controlled large areas of land west of the thirteen states. Other states, including Maryland and Rhode Island, did not hold any western land. Delegates worried that states such as Virginia would grow too powerful. They wanted those states to hand over their western land to the central government. But these states refused to give up their land. In the end, Congress agreed to let them keep their land.

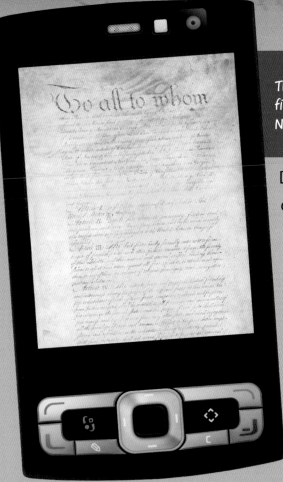

The Articles of Confederation were finally approved by the delegates on November 15, 1777.

Delegates from the smaller states did not like this plan. Even so, they agreed to it.

The debates over the Articles of Confederation lasted sixteen months. Finally, the delegates approved the document on November 15, 1777. But the next hurdle was going to be even harder. A copy of the Articles had to go to all thirteen states. And every single state had to approve the Articles. Only then would they become the law of the land.

NEXT QUESTION

WHY

DID THE STATES HAVE TROUBLE AGREEING TO THE ARTICLES OF CONFEDERATION?

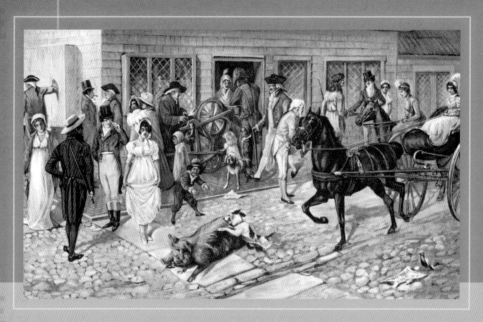

An artist painted this late 1700s street scene of colonial New York City. The states would have to come together to vote on the proposed Articles of Confederation.

THREE THE SQUABBLING STATES

The Continental Congress ordered three hundred copies of the Articles to be printed. The copies were sent to all the states. Delegates also included a letter with the document. In it they urged the states to |ratify| the Articles of Confederation no later than March 10, 1778.

to give official approval of

The lawmakers in each state began discussing the Articles. These leaders had to decide whether their state would ratify the document. Congress asked them to be "wise and patriotic." It pleaded with them to focus on the needs of their new nation.

WHAT DID THE COUNTRY DO WITHOUT AN OFFICIAL GOVERNMENT?

From 1775 to 1781, the Continental Congress unofficially ran the country. The Articles of Confederation weren't ratified until 1781. But the Congress still followed its rules. The Congress also organized the Continental Army. The Congress chose General George Washington of Virginia to lead the army. And it requested funds, soldiers, and supplies from the states.

The Articles of Confederation was "essential to our very existence as a free people," Congress said. "Without it, we may soon be [forced to say good-bye] to independence, to liberty, and safety." The states had to work together to win their freedom from Britain.

But state lawmakers had a hard time putting their new country first. Like most citizens, they were much more loyal to their state. In fact, when most Americans spoke of their country or nation, they were actually talking about their state.

Americans did not yet see themselves as one people. The states behaved more like the nations of Europe. They shared borders, but the citizens of each state felt very separate from those in other states.

This feeling of separateness made it hard for the states to trust one another. So ratifying the Articles was a great challenge. The states stalled for nearly three years. The country's leaders pleaded with them to put their differences aside.

John Witherspoon reminded the states why they needed the Articles. The states didn't just need a government to win the war, he said. They needed a government for *after* the war. He knew the states would disagree from time to time. Without a central government, those disagreements might turn into another war. He worried it would be "a more lasting war, a more unnatural, more bloody and much more hopeless war, among [the states]."

The message got through. By 1779 twelve states had ratified the Articles. Maryland alone refused. It ratified the document only after Virginia agreed to give up its western territories. Maryland became the final state to ratify the Articles on March 1, 1781.

At last the states were joined together as one nation. This event seemed like a miracle to many leaders. John Adams of Massachusetts exclaimed, "Thirteen clocks were made to strike together." He was amazed that such separate states could chime like a single clock.

John Adams

"Thirteen clocks were made to strike together."

The brand-new U.S. government was known as the Confederation Congress. This group of state delegates met to vote on important decisions for the country.

Each state was allowed to send two to seven delegates. A state's lawmakers chose how many delegates to send. They also chose who their delegates would be. Together, the delegates voted as a single group. Each state got one vote, even if it had many delegates.

The Confederation Congress met in several locations over the years. During their first two years (1781–1783), delegates met at Independence Hall in Philadelphia.

The delegates were expected to follow the wishes of their state's leaders. They debated and voted on issues facing the country. Major decisions needed the vote of at least nine states. An amendment to the Articles would need the approval of all thirteen states.

an addition or a change to a legal document

The Congress had the power to choose three officers to help run the government. The superintendent of finance took care of the nation's money. The secretary of war helped plan the war against Britain. And the secretary of foreign affairs built relationships with friendly nations.

the management, or handling, of how money is spent and saved

a person who runs a department of government

But these officers had very little power. The officers needed the delegates' approval to take action. The delegates voted on all important decisions.

The Articles also called for a president of the Confederation Congress. The first president of Congress was Samuel Huntington. He had even less power than the officers. He simply led Congress's meetings. He couldn't join in any debates. He couldn't even vote. He didn't stay in this job for long either. The delegates had to choose a new president every year.

According to the Articles, Congress alone had certain powers. Only Congress could declare war, keep a navy, and form friendships with foreign nations. Only Congress had the authority to print and borrow money. It could also run a national mail service. And it could settle disagreements between the states. In comparison, the Articles gave the states

This is a pattern for two sides of a silver dollar coin issued by the Continental Congress in 1776. Individual states also minted their own currency (money). The Confederation Congress wanted a single, national currency to be used throughout the former colonies.

many more powers. The states' greatest powers included taxing citizens and passing laws. States also had the right to punish people who broke their laws. This imbalance between the states and the central government put the country on a bumpy road. Until it could raise money and get its finances in order, the central government would remain weak.

NEXT QUESTION

WHO BECAME CONGRESS'S FIRST SUPERINTENDENT OF FINANCE?

George Washington *(center)*, leader of the Continental Army, asked delegates *(left)* to raise more money for his soldiers *(right)* during the war.

FOUR LIFE UNDER THE ARTICLES

Throughout the Revolutionary War, the Continental Army had been in trouble. It never had enough food, clothing, or medicine. Thousands of soldiers died from wounds, disease, or starvation. By 1781 those problems were worse than ever. General George Washington pleaded with the Confederation Congress for help.

Congress asked the states to send their fair share of money and soldiers. But the states gave much less than Congress had asked for.

The Confederation Congress grew desperate. It asked the states to send flour, corn, and meat instead of money.

That way it could at least feed the army. Congress even said it would take tobacco. It could sell this valuable crop to help pay for the war. But the states still sent barely enough supplies to keep the war going.

To help solve its money troubles, Congress chose its first superintendent of finance. His name was Robert Morris. This Philadelphia businessman went to work right away. He asked Congress for permission to create a national bank. The bank helped Morris keep better track of the nation's money. It was also the source of the government's printed paper money. The money helped fund the war.

Morris also demanded that the states start paying their fair share. But the states refused. He met with state lawmakers and leaders. He wrote letters to governors and other important people. He pushed, prodded, and bullied. He begged and scolded. He did everything he could to convince the states to give more.

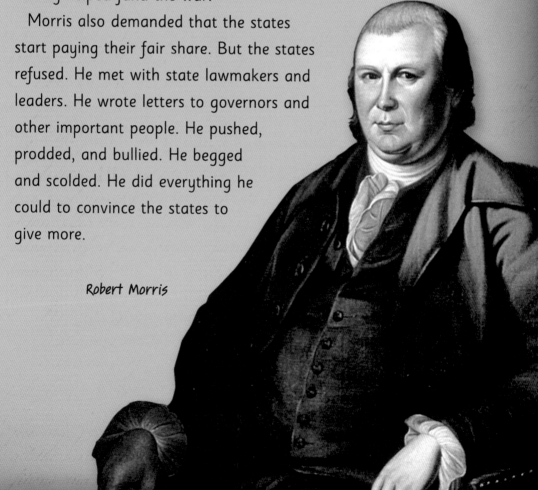

Robert Morris

The states told him they were doing their best. They complained that they had barely enough money and supplies for themselves. But Morris did not accept their excuses.

"What in the name of Heaven can be expected by the people of America but absolute ruin?" he asked. "How is our country to be defended? How is our army to be supported?" But no one paid attention to his desperate pleas. "It is like preaching to the dead," he grumbled in frustration.

Morris argued that Congress needed more power. It should use its army to force states to pay, he said. He also thought Congress should have the power to tax citizens directly. That way, paying for the war wouldn't depend only on the states' governments.

> "What in the name of Heaven can be expected by the people of America but absolute ruin? How is our country to be defended? How is our army to be supported?"
> —Robert Morris, July 9, 1782

Morris and other leaders wanted to add new amendments to the Articles of Confederation. These amendments would give Congress the powers it needed. But the delegates from all thirteen states had to vote for the amendments first.

Getting all the states to agree to the changes proved impossible. New amendments always failed. Meanwhile, the states continued to send less than Congress needed. The country was forced to turn to friendly nations such as France, the Netherlands, and Spain. It borrowed large amounts of money from these nations.

Despite these problems, the country won the Revolutionary War. In 1783 the United States of America signed the Treaty of Paris with Great Britain. This agreement officially gave the United States its independence. It also gave the nation much additional land.

a written agreement that sets out terms for peace

The country no longer had to keep a costly army. But its money problems were far from over. The nation struggled with huge debt. Congress needed to pay back the money it had borrowed from foreign nations. It also owed earnings to its army. After years of fighting, many soldiers had not been paid. Congress depended on the states to help with these debts.

money owed

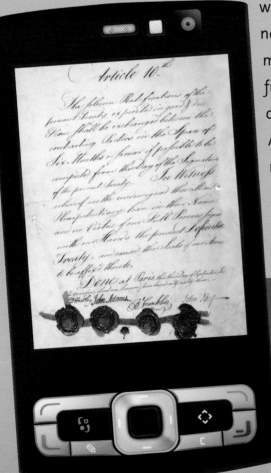

On September 3, 1783, the Treaty of Paris was signed by King George III and men who signed in the name of the Confederation Congress. It officially ended the Revolutionary War and freed the United States from Britain.

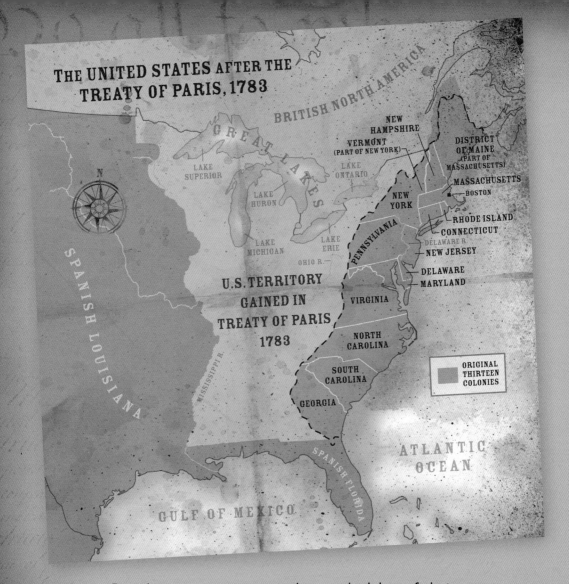

THE UNITED STATES AFTER THE TREATY OF PARIS, 1783

BRITISH NORTH AMERICA

GREAT LAKES

LAKE SUPERIOR

LAKE HURON

LAKE MICHIGAN

LAKE ONTARIO

LAKE ERIE

OHIO R.

NEW HAMPSHIRE

VERMONT (PART OF NEW YORK)

DISTRICT OF MAINE (PART OF MASSACHUSETTS)

MASSACHUSETTS

BOSTON

NEW YORK

RHODE ISLAND

CONNECTICUT

DELAWARE R.

NEW JERSEY

PENNSYLVANIA

DELAWARE

MARYLAND

U.S. TERRITORY GAINED IN TREATY OF PARIS 1783

VIRGINIA

NORTH CAROLINA

SOUTH CAROLINA

GEORGIA

SPANISH LOUISIANA

MISSISSIPPI R.

SPANISH FLORIDA

ATLANTIC OCEAN

GULF OF MEXICO

ORIGINAL THIRTEEN COLONIES

the lawmaking bodies of a government

But the states were struggling with debts of their own. To pay them off, state legislatures passed new taxes. Suddenly citizens were expected to pay their state government a lot more money. But many Americans were too poor to pay such high taxes. The war had caused money troubles for them too.

Before the war, Americans had sold many of their crops and products to Great Britain. In return, Britain sold British goods

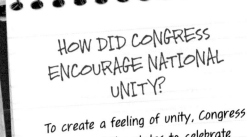

HOW DID CONGRESS ENCOURAGE NATIONAL UNITY?

To create a feeling of unity, Congress encouraged the states to celebrate the Fourth of July. Honoring the country's day of independence was a good way to bring Americans together. It reminded them of their shared victory against Britain.

to the colonies at low prices. This agreement allowed the colonies to prosper. That all changed after the war.

Great Britain stopped buying much from the United States. U.S. farmers and businesses had lost their main buyer. There just weren't enough people in the United States to sell to. Britain also raised the prices on the goods it sold to the United States. These changes made life hard for many Americans.

The country desperately needed to start trading with other nations. Congress tried to set up agreements for buying and selling goods. But the states argued over the best way to set up these agreements. Without the cooperation of the states, Congress's hands were tied. Americans had nowhere to sell their products. That caused much suffering for people.

Some states began punishing people who did not pay their taxes. Court judges ordered these citizens to sell their property. Money from the sale went to the state. This use of power outraged the poorest citizens. Angry mobs formed in places such as Connecticut and New Hampshire. The mobs attacked and shut down courts.

Farmers were angry that states had raised taxes after the war. In Massachusetts, Daniel Shays *(left)* and Job Shattuck *(right)* led a violent protest called Shays's Rebellion. This picture of the two men ran in *Bickerstaff's Boston Almanack for 1787.*

In Massachusetts a farmer named Captain Daniel Shays led a violent protest. Like many soldiers, he was still waiting to be paid for his service in the war. Early in 1787, he and about two thousand men marched into Springfield, Massachusetts. They tried to steal government weapons that were stored there. This event became known as Shays's Rebellion.

resistance, often armed, against an authority such as a government

The leaders of Massachusetts were worried. Shays's men might do real harm. Massachusetts wanted Congress to send an army to stop the violence. But Congress had no money for an army. Instead, Massachusetts paid some of its own men to put an end to the attack.

Shays's Rebellion rang an alarm bell throughout the country. People feared that more violent rebellions might spring up in other places. The rebellions might turn into battles or even wars. The country needed money to keep an army.

Not having an army also made the country look weak to other nations. Both Britain and Spain controlled land along U.S. borders. These countries knew the United States had no way to protect itself. So they tried to take control of parts of the country.

Some U.S. leaders began calling for big changes. They argued that the Confederation's weak government wasn't working. These men were known as federalists. They called for a powerful central, or federal, government. During all the turmoil, the population of the states continued to increase. Without a stronger government, the federalists warned, the United States might fall apart.

SHAYS'S REBELLION
This modern-day map shows the routes of Shay's rebels.

MASSACHUSETTS

Connecticut River

Northampton

to Boston →

Holyoke

Chicopee

Springfield

CONNECTICUT

GPS

NEXT QUESTION

WHERE DID SOME AMERICANS MOVE AS THE COUNTRY'S POPULATION GREW?

Settlers heading westward camp for the night on the prairie. The growing country had many decisions to make about how the government should act for the settlers.

FIVE AN ENDING AND A BEGINNING

Not everyone agreed with the federalists. Many U.S. leaders disliked the idea of a powerful central government. These men were called antifederalists. They wanted to guard the power of the states.

At the same time, many states were losing interest in the Confederation Congress. Said Thomas Jefferson, "The constant session of Congress can not be necessary in times of peace." Sometimes the states barely sent enough delegates to vote on important decisions. They also sent less and less money to Congress. The country's money problems continued to worsen. Meanwhile its population continued to grow.

By early 1787, even antifederalists agreed that the Articles of Confederation needed some changes. Congress should be able to pass certain taxes. It also needed to set up agreements for trading with foreign nations. Otherwise, the country would continue to suffer.

In February the Confederation Congress approved a convention. According to Congress, the convention's delegates would have "the sole and express purpose of revising the Articles of Confederation." Their job would be to agree on a few amendments to the Articles.

a large meeting of people with a common purpose

The convention took place in Philadelphia in May 1787. It later became known as the Constitutional Convention. This convention brought together delegates from all the states except Rhode Island. One of those delegates was John Dickinson. Although he was aging and ill, he wanted to take part in this important event. Robert Morris also attended the convention.

George Washington addresses the Constitutional Convention in 1787. This scene was painted by American artist Junius Brutus Stearns (1810–1885).

As usual, all thirteen states had to approve any amendment to the Articles. And as usual, getting everyone's approval seemed like an impossible task. Federalists quickly suggested a different idea. Why not write a constitution? they asked. This new document would set down rules for a new federal government.

With a fresh start, the convention's delegates could also set new rules for ratifying the Constitution. They would no longer need the votes of thirteen states. Instead, they could ask for the approval of two-thirds, or nine, of the states. The delegates agreed to consider the idea.

Virginia was the first state to share its plan for a federal government. A strong federalist named James Madison had written much of it. His Virginia Plan gave the government much more power than the Articles of Confederation had. It also called for a powerful three-part government.

James Madison

This government would replace the weak Confederation Congress.

In response, antifederalists presented the New Jersey Plan. This plan was almost the same as the Articles of Confederation. But it gave Congress a bit more power. The delegates began debating the strengths and weaknesses of these two plans.

While the Constitutional Convention delegates debated, the Confederation Congress was still hard at work. It had set up rules for the expanding western territories.

The country's population had grown a lot since the war. Many Americans were moving westward from the states to the territories. Congress knew it had to treat the territories fairly. Otherwise, the territories might break free from the United States.

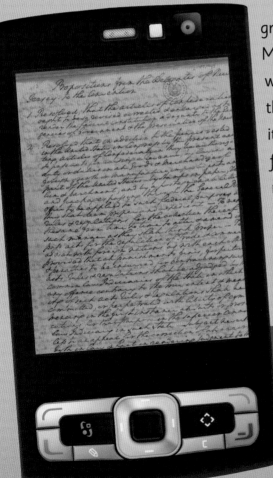

This is a copy of the New Jersey Plan. The plan was given to the Constitutional Convention as an alternative to the plan put forth by James Madison of Virginia.

On July 13, 1787, Congress approved the Northwest Ordinance. It gave citizens in the western territories the same rights as those in the states. The ordinance gave a new territory the right to its own government. It also said that any territory could become a state if its population reached sixty thousand. All new states would be "on an equal footing with the original States in all respects whatever." The original thirteen states would have no greater power than new states.

The Northwest Ordinance made another important rule. It said that slavery was not allowed in any western territory. At the time, slavery existed in all the southern states. It was also allowed in most of the northern states. The Northwest Ordinance was one of the greatest successes of the Confederation Congress. It allowed the country to grow and prosper.

Later that summer, the Constitutional Convention also made an important decision. Its delegates agreed on most of the ideas in Madison's Virginia Plan. This document became the U.S. Constitution. On September 17, 1787, the delegates signed the Constitution. But nine states still had to ratify it before the document became the official law of the land.

This bronze sculpture is in the U.S. Capitol Building in Washington, D.C. It portrays the signing of the U.S. Constitution.

Ratification happened less than a year later. Elections took place under the new Constitution in November 1788. Voters elected George Washington as the nation's first president. They also elected lawmakers to the U.S. Congress. The president and the lawmakers took office in March 1789.

Life under the Articles of Confederation had come to an end. But its accomplishments were long lasting. The work of the Confederation Congress allowed the nation to win the Revolutionary War. And its Northwest Ordinance benefited the country for years to come.

HOW IS THE FEDERAL GOVERNMENT STRUCTURED UNDER THE CONSTITUTION?

The Constitution (right) divides the federal government into three branches, or parts. The executive branch is headed by the nation's president. The legislative branch includes the nation's lawmaking bodies. These are the Senate and the House of Representatives. The Supreme Court and the federal courts make up the judicial branch. The Constitution gives these three branches separate but equal powers. This division is called the separation of powers. It means that one or two branches can stop another branch from misusing its power. This system is known as checks and balances. It protects citizens and states if any branch becomes too powerful.

We the People

Article 1

George Washington (center), the first U.S. president, took the oath of office in 1789, as pictured in this painting by U.S. artist Hy Hintermeister.

The Articles of Confederation had forced the states to work together. It united them as a single country. The Articles paved the way for the Constitution, the federal government, and the nation we have today.

NEXT QUESTION

HOW DO WE KNOW ABOUT THE ARTICLES OF CONFEDERATION?

Primary Source: Notes from Thomas Jefferson

We know about the Articles of Confederation from writings of the time. These papers are important primary sources. A primary source is a document written by a person who was alive at the time of an event. It is often a firsthand description of something that happened in history. Letters, journals, and newspaper articles are examples of primary sources. The primary source below comes from Thomas Jefferson's notes. It describes the early debates about how many votes each state should have in the Confederation Congress.

> July 30, 31, August 1. Present forty-one members. Mr. Chase observed this [issue] was the most likely to divide us. . . . [He said] that larger colonies had threatened they would not confederate at all, if their weight in Congress should not be equal to the numbers of people they added to the confederacy; while the smaller ones declared against a union, if they did not retain an equal vote for the protection of their rights. . . . He was of opinion, the smaller colonies would lose their rights, if they were not in some instances allowed an equal vote. . . .
>
> John Adams advocated the voting in proportion to numbers. He said that we stand here as the representatives of the people: that in some States the people are many, in others they are few; that therefore, their vote here should be proportioned to the numbers from whom it comes.

TELL YOUR STORY ABOUT THE ARTICLES OF CONFEDERATION

Imagine that you are a delegate to the Continental Congress. You are debating the Articles of Confederation. Perhaps you are keeping a personal record of the debates or describing them in a letter to a friend.

WHAT state are you from?

WHERE are the debates taking place?

WHEN did they begin?

HOW long have they been going on?

WHO wrote the draft of the Articles?

WHY are the delegates meeting?

WHAT are the main issues being debated?

USE **WHO, WHAT, WHERE, WHY, WHEN,** AND **HOW** TO THINK OF OTHER QUESTIONS TO HELP YOU CREATE YOUR STORY!

Timeline

1754

The French and Indian War begins.

1763

Great Britain wins the French and Indian War.

1765

Britain's Parliament passes the Stamp Act.

1767–1768

John Dickinson publishes his *Letters from a Farmer* to protest new taxes on the colonies.

1774

Great Britain sends soldiers to Boston to control protesters. Parliament also passes laws to punish Massachusetts. Colonists named these laws the Intolerable Acts.

In September the **Continental Congress** meets in Philadelphia for the first time to discuss how to respond to the actions of Great Britain.

1775

The Revolutionary War begins on April 19. The Continental Congress meets again in May. Benjamin Franklin presents his *Sketch of Articles of Confederation*.

1776

The Continental Congress meets in June to prepare the Declaration of Independence and the Articles of Confederation. The Continental Congress approves the Declaration but does not come to an agreement on the Articles.

1777

The Continental Congress meets throughout the year to debate the Articles of Confederation and other important issues. It approves the Articles on November 15 and sends copies to the states.

1781

Maryland is the last state to ratify the **Articles of Confederation** on March 1.

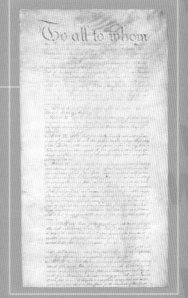

1783

The Revolutionary War officially ends. The United States signs the Treaty of Paris with Great Britain.

1787

The Confederation Congress approves the Northwest Ordinance. Delegates from twelve states gather in Philadelphia in May to discuss amendments to the Articles of Confederation. They approve a new document, the U.S. Constitution.

1788

Nine states ratify the Constitution, making it the official set of laws for the United States.

1789

The Constitution replaces the Articles of Confederation, and a new federal government comes to power.

Source Notes

11 Don H. Doyle and Marco Antonio Pamplona, eds., *Nationalism in the New World* (Athens: University of Georgia Press, 2006), 64.

12 Robert Middlekauff, *The Glorious Cause: The American Revolution, 1763–1789* (New York: Oxford University Press, 2005), 285.

13 Merrill Jensen, *The Articles of Confederation* (Madison: University of Wisconsin Press, 1940), 127.

14 *Articles of Confederation*, March 1, 1781, transcript, Yale Law School, Avalon Project, 2008, http://avalon.law.yale.edu/18th_century/artconf.asp (October 10, 2010).

16 Ibid.

17 "Continental Congress, Letter Transmitting Proposed Articles of Confederation," November 17, 1777, transcript, in *The Founders' Constitution* (Chicago: University of Chicago Press, 1986), 2000, http://press-pubs.uchicago.edu/founders/documents/v1ch7s4.html (October 10, 2010).

20 Ibid.

21 David C. Hendrickson, *Peace Pact: The Lost World of the American Founding* (Lawrence: University Press of Kansas, 2003), 141.

22 John Adams, *John Adams to H. Niles*, February 13, 1818, transcript, TeachingAmericanHistory.Org, 2008, http://teachingamericanhistory.org/library/index.asp?document=968 (October 10, 2010).

22 Ibid.

28 Ellis Paxson Oberholtzer, *Robert Morris: Patriot and Financier* (London: Macmillan Company, 1903), 132–133.

28 Ibid.

32 Ibid., 114.

34 Gordon S. Wood, *The American Revolution: A History* (New York: Modern Library, 2002), 148.

35 Colin Bonwick, *The American Revolution* (New York: Palgrave Macmillan, 2005), 231.

38–39 Confederation Congress, *The Northwest Ordinance*, July 13, 1787, transcript, Yale Law School, Avalon Project, 2008, http://avalon.law.yale.edu/18th_century/nworder.asp (October 10, 2010).

42 John P. Foley, ed., *Jeffersonian Cyclopedia: A Comprehensive Collection of the Views of Thomas Jefferson* (New York: Funk & Wagnalls Company, 1900), 973.

Selected Bibliography

Bonwick, Colin. *The American Revolution*. New York: Palgrave Macmillan, 2005.

Doyle, Don H., and Marco Antonio Pamplona, eds. *Nationalism in the New World*. Athens: University of Georgia Press, 2006.

Hendrickson, David C. *Peace Pact: The Lost World of the American Founding*. Lawrence: University Press of Kansas, 2003.

Jensen, Merrill. *The Articles of Confederation*. Madison: University of Wisconsin Press, 1940.

Middlekauff, Robert. *The Glorious Cause: The American Revolution, 1763–1789*. New York: Oxford University Press, 2005.

Wood, Gordon S. *The American Revolution: A History*. New York: Modern Library, 2002.

Further Reading and Websites

The American Revolutionary War
http://havefunwithhistory.com/HistorySubjects/AmericanRevolution.html
This website provides information about the war, as well as the events that came before it.

The Articles of Confederation
http://bensguide.gpo.gov/6-8/documents/articles/index.html
Learn about the contents of the Articles, and find links to images of the actual document.

The Declaration of Independence
Packed with information about this famous document, this kid-friendly website also has links to related games and activities.

DiPiazza, Francesca Davis. *When Did George Washington Fight His First Military Battle? And Other Questions about the French and Indian War*. Minneapolis: Lerner Publications Company, 2011. Follow George Washington from his first military battle until he became commander of the Continental Army.

Gondosch, Linda. *How Did Tea and Taxes Spark a Revolution? And Other Questions about the Boston Tea Party*. Minneapolis: Lerner Publications Company, 2011. Find out what those protesters in Boston were up to.

Ransom, Candice. *What Was the Continental Congress? And Other Questions about the Declaration of Independence*. Minneapolis: Lerner Publications Company, 2011. Learn how angry colonists decided to break free of British rule.

Ransom, Candice. *Who Wrote the U.S. Constitution? And Other Questions about the Constitutional Convention of 1787*. Minneapolis: Lerner Publications Company, 2011. Ransom explores the events that led to the writing of the Constitution, as well as the debates that took place during the Constitutional Convention.

Rosen, Daniel. *Independence Now: The American Revolution, 1763–1783*. Washington, DC: National Geographic, 2004. Rosen explores the history of the Revolutionary War.

LERNER SOURCE™

Expand learning beyond the printed book. Download free crossword puzzles, timelines, and additional website links for this book from our website, www.lerneresource.com.

Index

Photo Acknowledgments

The images in this book are used with the permission of: © iStockphoto.com/DNY59, p. 1; National Archives, pp. 1 (background) and all Articles of Confederation backgrounds, 19 (inset), 29 (inset), 40 (right), 45; © iStockphoto.com/sx70, pp. 3 (top), 7 (top), 9 (left), 15, 21, 31, 40 (left); © iStockphoto .com/Ayse Nazli Deliormanli, pp. 3 (bottom), 43 (bottom left); © iStockphoto.com/Andrey Pustovoy, pp. 4, 12, 19 (top), 29, 37; © age fotostock/SuperStock, p. 4 (inset); © Laura Westlund/Bill Hauser/ Independent Picture Service, pp. 4-5 (top), 30, 33 (inset), 38; © iStockphoto.com/Serdar Yagci, pp. 4–5 (background), 43 (background); © SuperStock/SuperStock, pp. 5, 9 (right), 35, 41 (top), 43 (bottom middle); © Everett Collection/SuperStock, p. 6; The Art Archive/General Wolfe Museum Quebec House/ Eileen Tweedy, p. 7 (bottom); The Art Archive, p. 8; The Granger Collection, New York, pp. 10, 12 (inset), 17, 27, 44; © North Wind Picture Archives, p. 11; Library of Congress, pp. 14 (LC-USZ62-49950), 16 (LC-USZ62-58593), 22 (LC-DIG-ppmsca-19162), 37 (inset); The Art Archive/Culver Pictures, p. 20; © MPI/Archive Photos/Getty Images, p. 23; © The Trustees of the British Museum/Art Resource, NY, p. 25 (top); © TopFoto/The Image Works, p. 26; © National Portrait Gallery, Smithsonian Institution/ Art Resource, NY, p. 32; © iStockphoto.com/Talshiar, p. 33 (top); © Hulton Archive/Getty Images, p. 34; © Universal Images Group/Hulton Archive/Getty Images, p. 36; © Stock Connection/SuperStock, p. 39.

Front cover: The Granger Collection, New York. Back cover: National Archives (background).

Main body text set in Sassoon Sans Regular 13.5/20. Typeface provided by Monotype Typography.